SURVIVAL GUIDE:

Strategies for Thriving in a
Competitive Market

Copyright Contents

TABLE OF CONTENT

Chapter 1: Navigating the Competitive Landscape

Introduction:

Surviving in a competitive market is a daunting task in today's ever-changing corporate scene. Entrepreneurs and company owners must manage a complicated web of elements that impact their operations to thrive. The first chapter of our "Survival Guide: Strategies for Thriving in a Competitive Market" is your guide to comprehending and mastering these essentials.

In this chapter, we'll take a look at the fundamental ideas that might mean the difference between just surviving and genuinely flourishing in a competitive market. We'll look at how to appraise your sector, identify your rivals, and react to the ever-changing market circumstances that define today's business environment. Let's unpack the complexities of this chapter, which establishes the groundwork for your company's competitive advantage.

Understanding the Dynamics of the Industry:

The first step in thriving in a competitive market is to properly comprehend the characteristics of your sector. Market size, growth patterns, the regulatory environment, and technological advances are all examples of industry dynamics. Understanding these dynamics allows you to see opportunities, predict problems, and modify your company plans appropriately.

Market Size and Future Growth Prospects:

Identifying the size and growth tendencies of the market in which you operate is a vital part of industry analysis. Is your industry growing, shrinking, or maintaining stability? These insights are critical for establishing realistic growth objectives and developing market entrance or development strategy. A thorough investigation and data analysis may offer a clear picture of where your sector stands.

Regulatory Framework:

Regulations may have a big influence on your company's operations. Understanding your industry's regulatory environment is critical for assuring compliance and avoiding legal stumbling blocks. Furthermore, these restrictions may generate or limit possibilities, making them an important consideration when developing your company plan.

Technological Progress:

Technology is critical in today's fast-paced corporate environment. Keeping up with technical changes might provide you with a competitive edge. Technology is frequently a driving factor for success, whether it's using cutting-edge technologies to optimize operations or harnessing creative solutions to fulfill client expectations.

Recognizing Competitor Analysis:

After you've obtained a full understanding of the dynamics of your industry, the next critical step is to examine your competitors. Knowing your rivals' strengths and shortcomings is critical for developing strategies that will set your company apart in a competitive market.

Identifying Competitors:

Begin by determining your direct and indirect rivals. Direct rivals provide equivalent goods or services to the same target market, while indirect competitors may provide alternatives or compete in neighboring areas. The first step in assessing the competitive environment is to identify your rivals.

Weaknesses and Strengths:

Evaluate your rivals' strengths and shortcomings thoroughly. What are their strong points, and where do they fall short? This study assists you in identifying chances to distinguish your company and provide higher value to consumers.

Positioning in the market:

Understanding your rivals' market positions is critical. Is it the market leader, a specialized specialist, or a newcomer? Understanding their viewpoints may help you make smart judgments. For example, if you're entering a market dominated by a few large players, you can think about focusing on a niche to avoid direct rivalry.

Customer Feedback:

Keep a careful eye on your rivals' consumer base. What kind of clients do they attract, and how loyal are they to them? **This data may assist you in tailoring your marketing and customer retention tactics to surpass your competitors.**

Market Trends and Conditions:

Keeping an eye on market conditions and trends is the last piece of the jigsaw while navigating the competitive environment. Change is the one constant in a dynamic corporate world, and being aware of these changes is critical for adapting and succeeding.

Economic Situation:

Consumer spending and corporate profitability may be influenced by economic factors such as inflation rates, interest rates, and general economic stability. Being aware of these situations may assist you in making sound financial choices.

Consumer Attitudes:

Consumer behavior and tastes are always changing. Understanding these changes, whether they are the result of cultural upheavals, technical improvements, or economic causes, is critical for changing your product or service offerings.

New Developments:

Emerging trends influence markets, which might be short-term fads or long-term developments. Keeping an eye on these trends enables you to develop and seize new chances. The emergence of sustainable and eco-friendly goods, for example, is a trend that firms in a variety of sectors have embraced.

Making Strategic Decisions in the Dark:

Navigating the competitive environment is more than simply obtaining information; it also entails turning that knowledge into sound strategic choices. Here are some pointers to help you make the most of this knowledge:

SWOT Evaluation:

Based on the insights gathered from industry analysis and competition research, do a SWOT analysis (Strengths, Weaknesses, Opportunities, Threats) for your firm. This tool may help you establish a clear strategic framework.

Strategy for Differentiation:

Create a differentiation plan based on the facts you have about your competition. Determine how you can differentiate yourself, whether via product innovation, exceptional customer service, or distinctive branding.

Adaptability and agility:

Market circumstances and trends may shift quickly. Your adaptability to these changes gives you a competitive edge. Maintain flexibility and be prepared to flip your plans as required.

Customer-First Approach:

Understanding consumer behavior and preferences enables you to take a customer-focused strategy. Tailor your goods, services, and marketing activities to your target audience's changing requirements and preferences.

Conclusion:

We've taken a tour through the fundamental concepts of prospering in a competitive market in this chapter. A good company plan is built on a thorough understanding of your industry, rivals, and market circumstances. It gives you the ability to make educated choices, react to changes, and ultimately position your company for long-term development and profitability.

As you go through this book, keep in mind that the information you obtain in this chapter will serve as the foundation for the methods and tactics you'll apply in later chapters. The competitive environment is ever-changing, and your ability to handle it successfully will decide your company's potential to not just survive but prosper. Maintain your curiosity, keep educated, and remain competitive.

Chapter 2: Crafting Your Unique Value Proposition

In a crowded and competitive economy, developing a distinct value proposition is critical to your company's success. It serves as the cornerstone for your marketing, customer interactions, and long-term success. In Chapter 2 of our "Survival Guide: Strategies for Thriving in a Competitive Market," we'll look at the complexities of developing a compelling value proposition that not only attracts but also keeps consumers coming back for more.

Your value proposition is the promise you make to your consumers. It explains the distinct advantages of your goods or services and why customers should choose you above the competition. In this chapter, we'll look at the art and science of establishing and communicating what makes your company unique. By the conclusion of this investigation, you will be well-equipped to create a value proposition that connects with your target audience and serves as the foundation of your marketing and commercial strategy.

Recognizing the Value Proposition:

A value proposition is simply a solution to the question, "Why should I choose your product or service over others?" It is the central statement that conveys the distinct value your company offers. To create a compelling value offer, you must first determine what sets your company apart from the competitors.

Identifying Your Unique Selling Points:

Identifying your distinct differentiators is the first step in developing your value proposition. What distinguishes your product or service? Superior quality, innovative features, great customer service, competitive price, or a combination of criteria might be considered. It is critical to understand your unique selling points.

Knowing Your Target Audience:

Your value offer should be personalized to your target audience's requirements, preferences, and pain areas. In today's economy, a one-size-fits-all strategy seldom works. Spend time getting to know your ideal consumers, their wants, and the difficulties your product or service addresses for them.

Advantages over features:

Your value proposition should emphasize the advantages that your clients will obtain. While features define what your product or service performs, benefits describe how it enhances the lives of your consumers. A smartphone's feature, for example, maybe its high-resolution camera, but the value is recording and sharing priceless experiences.

Making a Strong Value Proposition:

Now, let's look at how to create a compelling value proposition that connects with your target customer and distinguishes your company in a crowded industry.

Define Your Worth:

Begin by clearly identifying what your company provides that is important to clients. This comprises more than just product characteristics; it also includes the problem-solving capacity, convenience, or one-of-a-kind experience your offering gives.

Recognize Customer Needs:

To create a value offer that will entice clients, you must first understand their wants. Market research, surveys, comments, and consumer encounters all contribute to this insight. It's critical to match your value offer to what your clients genuinely want.

Highlight Your Distinctive Qualities:

What distinguishes you from the competition? Is it your knowledge, unique product features, or incomparable prices? Your value proposition should highlight these distinguishing characteristics.

Resolve Customer Issues:

Identify the pain areas that your target audience is experiencing and show how your product or service may remedy these issues. People are more inclined to pick a remedy that alleviates their discomfort.

Simplicity and clarity:

Keep your value offer simple and to the point. Avoid using jargon or unnecessarily complicated terminology. A dissatisfied consumer is unlikely to return to your company.

Benefits should be highlighted:

Emphasize the advantages of your offering. Explain how it improves, simplifies, or enhances your clients' lives. This emotional link has the potential to be a strong motivator.

Effective Value Proposition Examples:

Let's look at some real-world examples of value propositions that have successfully differentiated organizations in competitive markets:

Apple says, "Think Different."

Apple's value proposition focuses on innovation, design, and a one-of-a-kind customer experience. Their items are more than simply gadgets; they are instruments for personal expression and creativity.

"Get Fast, Free Shipping."

The value proposition of Amazon Prime is built on convenience and savings. It provides users with speedy shipment as well as access to a large library of entertainment and shopping possibilities.

Nike says, "Just Do It."

Nike's value proposition encourages people to be physically active and to accomplish their sports objectives. It's not only about the things; it's about a way of life and a way of thinking.

Zappos offers "365-Day Returns."

Zappos, an online shoe store, prioritizes customer service and convenience. Their value proposition guarantees clients an easy buying experience.

Tesla's slogan is "Sustainable Energy."

The value proposition of Tesla is founded on environmental sustainability and cutting-edge technology. Their electric vehicles are more than simply automobiles; they are part of a larger effort to cut carbon emissions.

Your value proposition does not have to be a single line, but it should be a concise and powerful statement that summarizes what your company stands for and what consumers can expect from you.

Developing Your Value Proposition:

Let's go through the processes of developing your distinct value proposition. This is not a one-time exercise, but rather a continual endeavor to develop and adapt as your company grows and the market changes.

Analysis and research:

Begin by researching your industry, competition, and target audience. This will offer you the fundamental insights required to develop a strong value proposition.

Determine your unique selling points:

What distinguishes your company? It might be a mix of product features, customer service, and cost. Make a list of your unique selling points.

Recognize Your Customers:

Invest in learning about your client's wants, needs, and pain areas. Surveys, interviews, and data analysis may all give useful information.

Value Proposition Statements in Draft:

Begin by developing several value proposition statements. These should be clear, succinct, and centered on the advantages your clients will gain.

Test and improve:

Test these assertions on a subset of your intended audience. Gather feedback and adjust your value offer in reaction to their comments.

Include Feedback:

Gather and implement client input regularly. Their perspectives will assist you in keeping your value offer current and engaging.

Continuity Across Channels:

Make sure your value proposition is consistent throughout all of your marketing platforms, including your website, social media, and advertising efforts.

Starbucks is a case study.

Let's look at a Starbucks case study to see how they've created a compelling value proposition that sets them apart in the competitive coffee sector.

Our Core Values: "Inspiring and Nurturing the Human Spirit - One Person, One Cup, and One Neighborhood at a Time."

Distinctive Differentiators:

Starbucks is more than simply coffee; it is an experience of a "third place" between work and home. Their in-store environment, high-quality drinks, and community emphasis set them apart.

Understanding the Needs of the Customer:

Starbucks understands that consumers want more than just coffee; they want a feeling of connection and belonging. This community demand is addressed in their value offer.

Solving Customer Issues:

Starbucks offers a comfortable setting for customers to mingle, work, or rest. These requirements are met by their offers, which include free Wi-Fi and comfy chairs.

Simplicity and clarity:

Starbucks' value proposition is simple. It's a promise that appeals to those looking for more than simply a cup of coffee.

Conclusion:

Creating a distinct value proposition is more than simply a marketing exercise; it is a critical component of your company strategy. Your value proposition articulates what your company stands for and why clients should do business with you. It's frequently the difference between striking out and fitting in in a competitive market.

We've gone over the fundamental elements of developing a compelling value proposition, from discovering differentiators to knowing your consumers and drafting clear and appealing statements. As you progress in your company, keep in mind that your value proposition will develop with it. Adapt and tweak it regularly to be current and attractive to your target audience.

Your value proposition is more than a statement; it is the foundation of your brand and the promise you make to your consumers. It's why they select you, stay with you, and become brand ambassadors. Your value proposition is your competitive advantage in a competitive market. Accept it, improve it, and allow it to steer your company to long-term success and prospering.

Chapter 3: Marketing Mastery

Marketing is the cornerstone that may push a firm to success or leave it floundering in obscurity in today's highly competitive business scene. The third chapter of our "Survival Guide: Strategies for Thriving in a Competitive Market" delves into the complicated and dynamic realm of marketing. In this section, we will look at the strategies, methods, and tactics that may help your company not just survive but flourish in a highly competitive market.

Marketing is more than simply promoting your goods or services; it is about knowing your consumers, producing value for them, and conveying that value effectively. In this chapter, we'll look at several aspects of marketing, from digital marketing in the Internet age to the continuing efficacy of classic marketing methods. By the conclusion of this trip, you'll be able to create and implement a thorough marketing strategy that will set your company apart from the competitors.

Marketing's Changing Landscape:

Marketing has progressed far beyond conventional print advertising and billboards. It now comprises a variety of channels and techniques, each with its own set of possibilities and problems. It is critical to adapt to the ever-changing marketing environment to succeed in a competitive market.

Dominance in the Digital Age:

The Internet and digital technology have transformed how organizations reach and connect with their customers. Social media, search engine optimization (SEO), email marketing, content marketing, and online advertising are all examples of digital marketing channels. These channels provide low-cost, highly focused methods to communicate with prospective consumers.

The King of Content:

Content marketing has developed as a very effective method. Providing quality, relevant, and educational material not only engages your audience but also establishes your company as an industry expert. Blog posts, videos, infographics, and podcasts are just a few types of material that may help you establish your brand and attract clients.

Decisions Based on Data:

Modern marketing is built on data analytics and customer insights. They enable organizations to make educated judgments and adjust their tactics to their target audience's demands and preferences. Marketing has become a more accurate and successful undertaking because of the capacity to gather and analyze data.

The Social Media Revolution:

Many firms now communicate with their customers via social media sites. These platforms allow for interaction, content exchange, and the development of a community around your business. Platforms such as Facebook, Instagram, Twitter, and LinkedIn provide companies with unique chances to display their goods and services.

Mobile Marketing with E-commerce:

Mobile marketing has become more crucial as e-commerce has grown. Because many customers increasingly purchase and engage with businesses via their smartphones and tablets, optimizing your website and marketing materials for mobile devices is critical.

Traditional Marketing Techniques:

While digital marketing has taken center stage, conventional marketing tactics remain viable and may be effective instruments in a full marketing strategy.

Print Marketing:

Traditional print media such as magazines, newspapers, brochures, and direct mail may still be useful, especially in specialized markets. These might provide a concrete and memorable manner of reaching out to targeted populations.

Television and radio commercials:

Television and radio advertising may reach a large number of people and give a visual or aural impact that digital media cannot match. They are, however, costly and may need precise targeting to achieve a decent return on investment.

Outdoor Advertising and Billboards:

Billboards and outdoor advertising may give excellent exposure, particularly in high-traffic regions. They may be especially useful for local firms trying to increase brand recognition.

Events and networking:

In-person networking and events enable companies to engage with consumers and other businesses in person. Trade exhibitions, conferences, and local events may be beneficial in terms of developing contacts and generating leads.

Marketing via Referral:

Word-of-mouth marketing is still a powerful force. Encourage pleased clients to suggest friends and family as a technique to attract new consumers.

Creating Your Marketing Strategy:

An effective marketing strategy does not include mindlessly throwing money at advertising. It's a well-planned and strategic strategy that corresponds with your company's objectives, target audience, and budget. The following are the essential phases in developing an efficient marketing strategy:

Set specific objectives:

Begin by outlining your marketing goals. Do you want to raise brand exposure, generate more leads, increase revenue, or enhance client retention? Your marketing approach will be guided by certain aims.

Understand Your Audience:

Understanding your intended audience is critical. Make comprehensive buyer personas to help you see and sympathize with your prospective consumers. This understanding will guide your messaging and channel choices.

Budget Distribution:

Determine how much money you can devote to marketing. The extent of your campaigns will be influenced by your budget, so be realistic about what you can afford.

Choosing a Channel

Choose the most relevant marketing channels based on your target demographic and objectives. For example, if your target demographic is active on Instagram, it may make sense to concentrate your efforts there.

Strategy for Content:

Create a content plan that addresses your target audience's pain areas and interests. Customers will be attracted and retained by high-quality, useful, and entertaining content.

Frequency and consistency:

Marketing relies heavily on consistency. Make certain that your message and branding are consistent across all mediums. Determine how often you will post content or perform ad campaigns.

Analysis and measurement:

Implement monitoring and analytics solutions to track the success of your marketing campaigns. Analyze the data regularly to fine-tune your plans.

Innovation and adaptation:

Prepare to respond to market and customer behavior changes. In a competitive market, innovation is often a critical difference.

The Marketing Power of Storytelling

Storytelling is an essential component of good marketing. It's not just about selling a product or service; it's about engaging on a deeper level with your audience. Storytelling may help you stand out from the crowd and develop a distinctive brand identity.

Developing a Brand Narrative:

Create an engaging brand narrative that conveys your beliefs, goal, and the consumer issue you're addressing. Spread this story across your marketing materials.

Customer Testimonials:

Distribute success stories and client feedback. Real-life examples of how your product or service has benefited individuals might help you create trust and confidence.

Resonating Content:

Telltales that are meaningful to your target audience. Understand their difficulties, goals, and values, and then produce content that answers them.

Emotional Attachment:

Make an emotional connection with your audience by using storytelling. Emotions are strong motivators of customer behavior. Emotional stories may be really powerful.

Authenticity:

Be genuine in your tale. Authenticity fosters trust. To develop a more authentic relationship with your audience, share both your triumphs and your problems.

Case Study: Nike's "Just Do It"

Nike's marketing exemplifies the power of narrative in branding. "Just Do It," their popular tagline, symbolizes their brand's attitude, which is built on pushing individuals to overcome obstacles and accomplish their objectives. The tagline sells more than simply shoes; it promotes a way of thinking and living.

Nike tells the tales of ordinary people and sportsmen who have pushed their limitations to achieve greatness via stunning advertisements and campaigns. These are tales about the human spirit, dedication, and achievement, not simply the product. Nike's lasting success is due in large part to the emotional connection it builds via its narrative.

Marketing Success Evaluation:

The performance of your marketing initiatives must be measured, just like any other company strategy. Effective measurement gives insights into what is working, what needs to be improved, and where additional resources should be allocated. Marketing success is measured using key performance indicators (KPIs).

Website Visits and Engagement:

Keep track of how many people visit your website and how they interact with it. Are they spending time on your website, responding to your calls to action, and becoming leads or customers?

Rates of Conversion:

Calculate the proportion of visitors who complete a desired activity, such as making a purchase, completing a contact form, or subscribing to your newsletter.

CAC (Customer Acquisition Cost):

Determine the cost of acquiring a new client via your marketing activities. This indicator is essential for determining the effectiveness of your marketing expenditure.

Customer Loyalty and Retention:

Customer loyalty and retention rates should be measured. Returning clients are often more important than new ones. Examine the effectiveness of your efforts to keep consumers interested and returning.

Metrics for Social Media

Track data like as followers, engagement (likes, comments, shares), and click-through rates, depending on the social media networks you use. These indicators may provide information about your social media influence.

Email Marketing Efficiency:

Examine your email campaigns' open rates, click-through rates, and conversion rates. Email marketing is still a powerful tool for engaging customers.

ROI (Return on Investment):

Determine your marketing initiatives' return on investment. Determine the income earned by marketing efforts about the expense of such operations.

Customer Surveys and Feedback:

Gather consumer feedback via surveys, reviews, and direct conversation. Their insights may supplement quantitative measurements with qualitative data.

The information gleaned from these measurements should be used to influence your marketing approach. If a campaign or channel is underperforming, reallocate resources or make changes to increase its efficacy.

Conclusion:

Marketing is a dynamic and varied subject that is critical to a company's success in a competitive market. Whether you're embracing the digital era with online advertising and content marketing or relying on conventional techniques like print advertising and events, your marketing efforts should be guided by a thorough grasp of your target demographic and the objectives you've established.

We've discussed the shifting environment of marketing, the necessity of narrative, and the important stages in establishing a successful marketing strategy throughout this chapter. We've also spoken about how to track the performance of your marketing activities and utilize data to improve your plans.

Marketing expertise entails more than simply marketing your goods or services; it entails forging real relationships with your target audience, providing value, and standing out in a crowded marketplace. You may flourish and achieve long-term success in a competitive market by constantly adjusting and improving your marketing methods.

Chapter 4: Financial Fitness

Financial wellness is not a luxury in today's intensely competitive corporate market; it is a basic need. Even the most promising companies might fail due to poor financial management. The fourth chapter of our "Survival Guide: Strategies for Thriving in a Competitive Market" delves into the complexity of efficiently managing your business's finances. This chapter provides you with the financial knowledge you need to maintain the stability and development of your firm, from budgeting and cash flow management to getting capital.

Financial wellness is the foundation of a successful company. It entails not just keeping your financial house in order, but also strategically allocating your resources to achieve your objectives. In this chapter, we'll look at the fundamentals of financial health, such as how to build and maintain a budget, efficiently manage cash flow, and negotiate the sometimes-complicated process of accessing finance when it's required.

The Value of Financial Fitness:

Financial health is not a nebulous term. It's the foundation for your company's stability and success. Here's why it matters in a competitive market:

Sustainability:

Sound financial management guarantees that your company can survive in the long run. Without adequate financial preparation, you may find it difficult to meet bills and stay afloat.

Growth:

To flourish in a competitive market, you must often invest in expansion. Growth necessitates financial resources, whether it is growing your product range, entering new markets, or scaling your operations.

Risk Reduction:

Effective financial management reduces risks. A financial cushion may help your company weather unanticipated obstacles like economic downturns or industry upheavals.

Investor Satisfaction:

When seeking external funds or partners, proving financial soundness gives investors or stakeholders trust. They want to know that their money is being handled carefully.

Making a Sound Budget:

Creating a detailed budget is one of the first steps toward financial wellness. A budget is more than simply a financial plan; it is your financial success roadmap. It enables you to properly manage resources, track your progress, and make educated choices. Let's look at the important components of making a sound budget:

Revenue Estimates:

Begin by predicting your income for the next quarter. This should be based on previous data, market research, and sales projections. If relevant, think about various income sources.

Category of Expenses:

Identify and classify your spending. Operating expenditures (rent, utilities, wages), variable costs (materials, shipping), and any one-time or special expenses (e.g., marketing campaigns) are examples of these.

Cost-cutting measures:

Set spending limits for each cost category. These are the funds you have budgeted for. They should be practical and in line with your financial objectives.

Monitoring regularly:

Your budget is a living document, not a static one. Compare your real income and spending to your budget regularly. This helps you see any differences and make any required changes.

Emergency Reserve:

Set aside a percentage of your money in your budget to create an emergency fund. This fund acts as a safety net in the event of unforeseen costs or economic downturns.

Examine and revise:

Review your budget regularly to verify that it is still in line with your company's financial goals. Make the appropriate modifications if your company's conditions change.

Effective Cash Flow Management:

Your company's cash flow is its lifeline. It refers to the influx and outflow of cash in your business. Effective cash flow management is critical to ensuring you have the liquidity to meet expenditures, invest in growth, and capitalize on opportunities. Here are some methods for maintaining a good cash flow:

Payment Collection and Invoicing on Time:

Send out invoices as soon as possible, and follow up on outstanding bills. Encourage clients to pay on time by giving early payment incentives or instituting late fines for late payments.

Negotiations with the vendor:

Negotiate advantageous arrangements with your suppliers. This might include things like longer payment periods or volume discounts. These discussions may help you handle your incoming cash flow more effectively.

Cash Flow Projection:

To foresee times of excess or deficit, create a cash flow projection. This helps you to prepare ahead of time, such as putting money away during high-revenue months to meet costs during low-revenue months.

Expense Management:

Keep a close eye on your spending and search for ways to save money without losing quality or service. Small, recurrent costs may frequently pile up and influence cash flow.

Credit Availability:

Consider getting a credit line or a company credit card for emergencies. When required, they may offer short-term financial alternatives.

Inventory Control:

Manage your inventory effectively to prevent overstocking or running out of important products.

Inventory management has a direct influence on cash flow.

Obtaining Funding:

While sound financial management may go a long way, there are instances when external capital is required for expansion, innovation, or overcoming financial issues. Understanding the many sources of finance and how to acquire them is a crucial ability in a competitive industry.

Bootstrapping:

Many entrepreneurs self-fund their firms, often known as bootstrapping. This strategy entails combining personal savings and company earnings to support operations and growth. It gives you complete control but may restrict the scope of your actions.

Debt funding:

Debt financing entails borrowing money from financial institutions such as banks, credit unions, and internet lenders. Company loans, lines of credit, and company credit cards are all common kinds of debt financing. Debt finance may offer a speedy infusion of funds, but it often involves interest-bearing repayment.

Equity Investment:

Selling a piece of your company to investors in return for funds is what equity financing entails. Angel investors, venture capitalists, and even friends and family might be among these investors. While this method does not incur debt, it does require a certain amount of control and ownership.

Crowdfunding:

Crowdfunding systems enable you to raise funds from a large number of people, sometimes in the form of tiny individual donations. This might be an interesting choice for product development or creative endeavors.

Grants and Contests:

Investigate grants, subsidies, and business contests with monetary awards. These possibilities may be industry, geography, or company model-specific.

Strategic Alliances:

Collaboration with existing corporations or organizations may give access to their networks, resources, and experience in addition to financial assistance.

Personal Assets and Savings:

Personal assets, or savings, are often used to support a company. This technique, however, entails personal financial risks.

Obtaining finance is not a one-size-fits-all endeavor. The financing strategy you choose is determined by your company's unique demands, stage, and the terms and circumstances you are willing to accept.

Increasing Financial Resilience:

Financial resilience is a competitive advantage in a competitive market. Financial resilience entails being able to resist economic shocks, adapt to changing market circumstances, and capitalize on opportunities as they emerge. Here are some financial resilience strategies:

Revenue streams should be diversified.

Relying on a single income source might expose your company to risk. Investigate diversification options, such as releasing new goods or services or targeting other client categories.

Emergency Reserve:

As previously said, having an emergency fund may give a financial buffer during difficult times. This money should ideally cover at least three to six months of operational expenditures.

Insurance:

Invest in commercial insurance to reduce hazards. This might include liability insurance, property insurance, or business interruption insurance, depending on your sector.

Planning for Continuity:

Create a business continuity strategy to guarantee that your company can continue to function in the face of interruptions caused by natural catastrophes, market movements, or unanticipated occurrences.

Retention of Customers:

Building excellent client connections may assist in maintaining a consistent flow of income, especially during difficult times. Customers that are pleased and loyal to your company are more inclined to return.

Margin of Profit:

Profit margins should be monitored and improved. A high-profit margin allows for the absorption of unforeseen expenditures as well as the investment in expansion.

Financial knowledge:

To ensure your financial management is optimal, get financial guidance from specialists such as accountants or financial advisers.

Apple's Financial Resilience as a Case Study

Apple is well-known for its inventive goods as well as its financial strength. The corporation has amassed a sizable financial reserve, known colloquially as a "war chest," throughout the years. This reserve offers financial certainty, allowing Apple to spend on R&D, grow product lines, and weather economic downturns.

Apple is not just financially resilient but also able to capitalize on opportunities such as acquisitions or investments in developing technology by retaining a strong cash reserve.

Conclusion:

Financial health is more than simply a business plan; it is a critical component of your company's existence and success. A strong financial management foundation helps you handle the unpredictability of a competitive market, develop a plan, and defend against unanticipated obstacles.

We've discussed the significance of financial health, the components of a sound budget, efficient cash flow management, and the numerous strategies for obtaining finance. Building financial resilience is about flourishing and long-term success in a competitive market, not simply surviving. Whether you're an experienced entrepreneur or just starting, mastering financial fitness is a talent that may set you apart from the crowd.

Chapter 5: Customer-Centric Strategies

Your customers are the lifeblood of your business. Learn how to build lasting relationships, provide exceptional customer service, and adapt to changing customer preferences.

In today's competitive business climate, your customers are more than simply purchasers; they are the lifeblood of your company. Their contentment, loyalty, and advocacy may be critical differentiators in your success path. Our "Survival Guide: Strategies for Thriving in a Competitive Market" devotes Chapter 5 to the art and science of customer-centric tactics. We discuss the significance of developing long-term connections, offering outstanding customer service, and responding to changing client preferences.

Customer-centricity is more than a slogan in today's corporate world; it's a fundamental way of conducting business. Customers have more options and more expectations than ever before, and companies that put them at the core of their operations prosper. This chapter delves into the different aspects of customer-centric strategies, such as appreciating the importance of customer connections, providing outstanding service, and being nimble in a fast-changing environment.

The Customer-Centric Advantage:

Customer-centricity entails orienting your company around your customers' requirements, preferences, and expectations. It all comes down to understanding that your consumers are the driving force behind your success. Here's why customer service is so important in a competitive market:

Retention of Customers:

Retaining current clients is often less expensive than acquiring new ones. An emphasis on customer-centric initiatives may aid in the development of loyalty and the retention of customers.

Word-of-Mouth Promotion:

Customers who are pleased with your services are your strongest advocates. They may boost your marketing efforts by sharing pleasant experiences with their friends and family, resulting in organic growth.

Advantage in Competition:

In a market where goods and services might be comparable, outstanding customer service and a customer-centric approach can help you stand apart.

Adaptability:

Client-centric firms react better to shifting client preferences and market situations. They keep in touch with their clients and may adjust as required.

Creating Long-Term Customer Relationships:

Customer connections that endure are the foundation of customer-centricity. These partnerships are built on trust, mutual understanding, and continuing value delivery, rather than one-time transactions. Here's how to establish and maintain these relationships:

Understand Your Customers:

Knowing your consumers intimately is the first step in developing long-term connections. Create thorough buyer personas or consumer profiles to better understand their requirements, desires, and problem areas.

Personalization:

When feasible, tailor your interactions and products to unique clients. Personalization shows that you regard their distinct tastes.

Communication that works:

Communication must be two-way. Listen to your consumers and have open, honest interactions with them. Solicit feedback and utilize it to make changes.

Consistency:

It is critical to maintain consistency in your goods, services, and interactions. Customers should know what to expect from your company every time they interact with it.

Surprising and delightful:

Go above and above to surprise and satisfy your consumers. Unexpected acts of gratitude may generate unforgettable memories.

Programs of Loyalty:

Implement loyalty schemes that encourage repeat purchases. These initiatives may entice consumers to return and make more purchases.

Excellent Customer Service:

Customer-centricity is defined by exceptional customer service. It is all about exceeding the expectations of customers. The following are the essential components of outstanding customer service:

Accessibility:

Ensure that your consumers may contact you via a variety of methods, such as phone, email, chat, or social media. Provide a consistent, responsive experience.

Empathy:

Customer service workers who are empathetic comprehend and care about the customer's issues. They do more than simply address problems; they make clients feel appreciated.

Quick Reaction:

It is critical to respond quickly. Recognize client requests and concerns as soon as possible, even if you need additional time to thoroughly handle the situation.

Problem Solving:

Concentrate on addressing difficulties effectively and efficiently. Customers value firms that can transform a bad experience into a good one.

Proactive communication:

Anticipate consumer demands and interact with them ahead of time. Send delivery updates, for example, or offer product use advice.

Education and empowerment:

Give your customer support personnel the training and authority they need to efficiently manage consumer complaints. Employees who are empowered may make choices that benefit consumers.

Changing Customer Preferences Adaptation:

Customer tastes and the corporate environment are always changing. Customer-centric firms are quick to respond to these changes. Here's how you keep up with changing client preferences:

Market Analysis:

Conduct market research regularly to keep current on consumer preferences, developing trends, and competition products. This information may help you plan your approach.

Loop of Feedback:

Make a feedback loop with your clients. Encourage them to provide recommendations and comments. Make educated judgments with this input.

Integration of Technology:

Accept technologies that may assist you in better understanding and catering to client preferences. Customer relationship management (CRM) systems, data analytics, and automation may be included.

Experimentation:

Be open to new ideas and experimentation. Test new products or marketing methods to assess how they are received by your target demographic.

Responsive customer service:

Customer service must be flexible. Respond swiftly and effectively to client issues and changing demands.

Continuous Education:

Maintain your curiosity and willingness to study. Attend professional conventions, read industry journals, and engage in the continued education of your personnel.

Amazon's Customer-Centric Approach Case Study

Amazon is a perfect example of a customer-focused company. The company's success has been driven by its emphasis on client happiness, convenience, and innovation. Here are a few examples of Amazon's customer-centric strategy:

Personalized Suggestions:

Amazon's recommendation engine uses customer data to propose goods that are likely to be of interest. Personalization improves the purchasing experience.

Membership in Prime:

Amazon Prime is a consumer loyalty club that provides perks such as free two-day delivery, streaming, and exclusive access to specials. It promotes client retention and repeat business.

Customer Feedback:

They include customer reviews in Amazon product listings. These evaluations serve as social evidence and assist buyers in making educated judgments.

Responsive customer service:

Customer service at Amazon is well-known for its timeliness and problem-solving abilities. The organization aims to handle difficulties swiftly and to the satisfaction of the client.

Innovation:

Amazon is continually innovating to satisfy the changing needs of its customers. This includes the launch of new services such as Amazon Fresh, which provides food delivery, and Amazon Web Services (AWS), which provides cloud computing.

Conclusion:

consumer-centric methods are not a one-size-fits-all strategy; they need a thorough grasp of your consumer base as well as a dedication to continually providing excellent experiences. These tactics are what may set your company apart and generate long-term success in a competitive industry.

Throughout this chapter, we've discussed the need for customer-centricity, the value of long-term connections, the components of excellent customer service, and the need to adapt to changing client preferences. Whether you're an experienced entrepreneur or just starting, understanding customer-centric methods is a talent that may help you flourish, develop, and achieve long-term success in today's dynamic and competitive economy.

Chapter 6: Innovation and Adaptability

In a competitive market, innovation and adaptability are key. Discover how to foster a culture of innovation and pivot your strategies when necessary to stay ahead of the competition.

Survival and success in the ever-changing corporate world are dependent on two critical characteristics: creativity and flexibility. In Chapter 6 of our "Survival Guide: Strategies for Thriving in a Competitive Market," we discuss cultivating an innovative culture and mastering flexibility. Here, we'll look at how to create an atmosphere conducive to innovation, as well as how to pivot your strategy as needed to remain one step ahead of the competition.

Innovation and flexibility are more than buzzwords in competitive marketplaces; they are the lifeblood of enterprises. Because of the rapid rate of change, the advent of new technologies, and altering client preferences, a proactive approach is required. This chapter delves into the complexities of these critical talents, from encouraging innovation inside your business to the art of quick adaptability.

The Importance of Innovation:

Innovation is more than simply generating new items; it is also about discovering better ways to do things, whether it is refining procedures, reinventing your business model, or improving the consumer experience. Here are some of the reasons why innovation is critical in a competitive market:

Competitive Advantage:

Innovative businesses often lead the pack. They bring new ideas, goods, and services to market, distinguishing themselves from competition.

Relevance in the market:

Staying relevant is crucial as market conditions alter. Innovation keeps your company in step with evolving client wants and expectations.

Solving Customer Issues:

Innovation enables you to handle client pain points more effectively, creating solutions that not only meet but exceed their expectations.

Gains in Efficiency:

Innovation may contribute to operational efficiency, cost reductions, and increased profitability.

Risk Reduction:

Diversifying your company via innovation. If one region has difficulties, other creative initiatives might function as a buffer.

Recruiting Talent:

Businesses that are recognized for their innovation often recruit top personnel. Creative people are attracted to companies that promote new ideas.

Creating an Innovative Culture:

Innovation is not restricted to a few; it is a culture that can be fostered inside a company. Here's how to develop an innovative culture:

Leadership Assistance:

The tone for innovation is established by leadership. From the top down, encourage and reward innovative thinking. Leaders must also be open to new ideas and take risks.

Experimentation Freedom

Create an atmosphere in which workers may experiment and take measured risks without fear of repercussions if they fail.

Diverse Groups:

Diverse viewpoints and ideas may result from team diversity. Diverse backgrounds and experiences may inspire creative ideas.

Collaboration:

Encourage cross-functional teamwork. Innovation often develops at the crossroads of diverse disciplines or skills.

Idea Generation Sessions:

Organize brainstorming sessions and platforms for idea exchange. Make a secure area for workers to communicate their ideas, even if they appear outlandish.

Loops of Feedback:

Implement new idea feedback methods. Constructive criticism may aid in the refinement of ideas and their progression toward implementation.

Rewards and recognition:

Recognize and recognize novel contributions. This might take the shape of monetary compensation, promotions, or just acknowledging a job well done.

Innovation Resources:

Allocate resources to promote innovation, whether it's specialized teams, R&D money, or access to innovative tools and technology.

Google's Innovation Culture as a Case Study

Google is well-known for its innovative culture. It began as a search engine and has now grown into a conglomerate with multiple companies, all of which demonstrate a dedication to innovation and disruption. Here are some examples of Google's innovative culture:

20% Time:

Google notably implemented the "20% time" policy, which encourages workers to spend 20% of their work hours on projects of their choice. This flexibility resulted in technologies such as Gmail and Google Maps.

Multidisciplinary Teams:

Google encourages multidisciplinary teamwork. Engineers, designers, and data scientists collaborate to solve challenging challenges and stimulate creativity.

Labs for Innovation:

Google has innovation laboratories devoted to moonshot initiatives, such as "X" (previously Google X), aiming for radical discoveries that might transform industries.

Culture Based on Feedback:

Google has a culture that appreciates feedback. Employees are encouraged to submit feedback on anything from goods to workplace practices, encouraging an open communication culture and the ability to learn from errors.

Adaptability in a Dynamic Environment:

Being adaptable is being quick to respond to change. The capacity to pivot when required in today's fast-paced corporate world might be the difference between succeeding and falling behind. Here are some of the reasons why adaptation is so important in a competitive market:

Customer Preferences Changing:

Customer preferences shift. Businesses must adapt their offers to reflect these trends.

Technological Progress:

Industries may be swiftly disrupted by technology. Adaptable businesses keep up with technological advances and use them to their advantage.

Market Trends:

Market circumstances might change. Adaptable businesses may exploit chances during upswings and protect themselves during downturns.

Competitive Environment:

At any point, new rivals might appear. Adaptable businesses are prepared to react to a changing competitive scenario.

Global Happenings:

Global events, such as economic crises or pandemics, may have far-reaching consequences. Businesses can manage these unexpected hurdles thanks to their adaptability.

Regulatory Shifts:

Regulations are subject to change, which may have an impact on how a corporation runs. Adaptable businesses remain compliant and alter their tactics appropriately.

Developing Adaptability:

Adaptability does not mean responding rashly to every change; it means being deliberate and prepared. Here's how to improve your adaptability:

Continuous Education:

Encourage a learning culture in your business. This might include training programs, seminars, or just cultivating a curious mentality.

Planning Scenarios:

Conduct scenario planning exercises to foresee possible future difficulties and find solutions.

Decision-Making Based on Data:

Make use of data and analytics to help you make choices. Data might provide information about shifting consumer behavior and market trends.

Cross-Functional Groups:

Cross-functional teams that bring together varied viewpoints and experiences may swiftly adjust to change.

Operational Flexibility:

Make your operations flexible and scalable. Outsourcing, cloud-based technology, and flexible personnel may all be used.

Management of Risk:

Implement risk management tactics that detect and prepare for possible hazards.

The Role of Leadership:

Leadership is critical in establishing the tone for adaptation. Leaders must be flexible and enable their people to adjust.

Netflix's Adaptability as a Case Study

Netflix is an outstanding example of flexibility. The firm started as a DVD-by-mail rental service, but as technology advanced, it swiftly shifted to streaming. It continues to evolve by creating original material, expanding into other markets, and providing new services like offline downloading. Despite early opposition from conventional cable providers, Netflix's agility enabled it to grow into a worldwide streaming behemoth.

Conclusion:

In a competitive market, adaptation and innovation are not merely techniques; they are the fundamental core of survival and success. These abilities enable organizations to not just flourish in a dynamic environment but also to shape it. Throughout this chapter, we've discussed the importance of innovation and adaptability, the art of cultivating an innovative culture, and the science of mastering adaptation. Whether you're an established company or a start-up, learning these abilities may be your passport to long-term success and prominence in today's ever-changing competitive scene.

Chapter 7: Sustainability and Long-Term Success

This final chapter explores sustainable business practices that will help your business thrive over the long term. From social responsibility to growth strategies, we'll guide you toward lasting success.

The last part of our "Survival Guide: Strategies for Thriving in a Competitive Market" goes into the world of sustainability and long-term success in the big tapestry of business. In this perspective, sustainability includes not just environmental responsibility but also social and economic sustainability. It is about ensuring that your company not only survives but also flourishes in the long run. In this chapter, we will look at sustainable business methods that can help you achieve long-term success.

Long-term success is the ultimate aim in a competitive market. Sustainability is more than simply guaranteeing your company's existence; it is also about maintaining its profitability for years to come. In this chapter, we'll look at the many aspects of sustainability, such as environmental stewardship, social responsibility, and growth methods that may lead to long-term success.

Sustainability's Multifaceted Nature:

Sustainability entails striking a balance across three critical dimensions: environmental, social, and economic. These elements are interrelated and constitute the cornerstone of a long-term company. Let's take a closer look at each one:

Environmental Longevity:

Environmental sustainability entails limiting your company's environmental effects. This includes resource stewardship, energy efficiency, waste minimization, and a dedication to combating climate change. Reduced greenhouse gas emissions, conservation of natural resources, and environmentally friendly behaviors are among the strategies.

Social Accountability:

Social sustainability includes your workers' well-being, the well-being of the communities in which you operate, and ethical supply chain management. Diversity and inclusion, fair labor standards, charity, and community participation are all part of it. Businesses that practice social responsibility actively aim to improve society.

Economic Persistence:

Economic sustainability refers to your company's long-term viability. It entails responsibly managing your funds, sustaining profitability, and assuring consistent growth. Investing in innovation, diversified income sources, and smart financial planning are all strategies.

The Value of Sustainability:

Sustainability is more than a corporate term; it is a basic strategy that reaps several advantages for both your company and society as a whole. Here are some of the reasons why sustainability is critical:

Brand Image and Reputation:

Sustainability activities improve the reputation of your brand. Customers choose companies that practice environmental and social responsibility.

Savings on costs:

Cost reductions are often the result of sustainability. Lower operating costs may be achieved via energy-efficient methods, waste reduction, and resource conservation.

Legal Obligation:

Environmental and labor standards must be followed by enterprises in many areas. You maintain compliance and decrease legal risks by adopting sustainability.

Risk Reduction:

Climate change, supply chain disruptions, and societal instability may all be mitigated by sustainability. A sustainable company is better suited to deal with these issues.

Recruiting Talent:

The younger generation emphasizes sustainability. Companies that commit to social and environmental responsibility attract more top talent.

Customer Satisfaction:

Customer loyalty may be increased via sustainability activities. Consumers are more inclined to stick with companies that share their beliefs.

Business Practices for Sustainability:

Now that we've established the characteristics and significance of sustainability, let's look at some sustainable business strategies that may contribute to long-term success:

Environmental Protection:

Energy Efficiency: Use energy-efficient methods such as LED lighting, optimizing heating and cooling systems, and using renewable energy sources such as solar power.

Reduce waste by recycling, reusing items, and implementing zero-waste practices.

Reduce your carbon footprint by using eco-friendly transportation, telecommuting, and procuring from sustainable sources.

Social Accountability:

Foster a diverse and inclusive environment that appreciates workers from all backgrounds.

Fair Labor Practices: Ensure that your supplier chain has fair salaries, safe working conditions, and ethical labor practices.

Community Engagement: Involve yourself in the areas in which you operate by participating in charity projects, volunteering, and forming community connections.

Economic Persistence:

Financial Planning: Create a strategic financial strategy to ensure your company's long-term stability and development.

Invest in innovation to remain competitive and to adapt to changing market circumstances.

Diversify your income sources to lessen your dependency on a single product or service.

Sourcing for Sustainability:

Ensure that your supply chain follows ethical and sustainable methods, from material procurement to manufacture and distribution.

Transparency and accountability:

Be open and honest about your sustainability initiatives. Report on your environmental, social, and economic sustainability measures regularly.

Accept sustainability standards and certifications to demonstrate your commitment to ethical business operations.

Strategies for Long-Term Growth:

Sustainability is more than simply preserving the status quo; it is also about ensuring that your firm develops responsibly and sustainably. Here are some sustainable growth tactics:

Sustainability Innovation:

Innovate while keeping sustainability in mind. Create environmentally sustainable, energy-efficient, and socially responsible goods and services.

The Circular Economy

Accept the circular economy paradigm, which emphasizes waste reduction and the reuse, recycling, or repurposing of resources and goods.

Expansion of the Market:

Expand into new markets that are consistent with your sustainability objectives. Look for opportunities where your environmentally friendly goods or services may flourish.

Strategic Alliances:

Collaborate with groups who share your dedication to sustainability. Partnerships may help you increase your influence and reach.

Acquisitions and mergers:

Consider mergers and acquisitions that are in line with your sustainability objectives. Acquiring companies with complementing sustainable practices may help you expand your offers.

Environmentally Friendly Technology:

Invest in technology that allows for environmentally friendly operations. Renewable energy technology, green logistical solutions, and energy-efficient equipment may be included.

Customer Training:

Inform your consumers about the environmental advantages of your goods or services. Well-informed customers are more inclined to purchase environmentally friendly choices.

Patagonia's Sustainability Journey Case Study

The outdoor apparel business Patagonia is well-known for its dedication to sustainability. The company's motto is "Build the best product, cause no unnecessary harm, use business to inspire and implement solutions to the environmental crisis." Patagonia's environmental efforts include the following:

Environmental accountability:

Making items out of recycled resources.

Committing to fair labor practices.

A portion of the revenues will be donated to environmental organizations.

Encourage consumers to repair and reuse items instead of purchasing new ones.

Transparency:

Providing information about its goods' environmental and social effects.

Encourage consumers to make educated decisions based on this knowledge.

Activism:

Taking a stance on environmental and social concerns, as well as leveraging the company's voice to promote change.

Conclusion:

Sustainability is a journey, not a destination. It is a dedication to long-term prosperity, accountability, and ethical business methods. Your firm may prosper in a competitive market while simultaneously contributing to a brighter future for everybody if it embraces sustainability in all of its aspects - environmental, social, and economic.

We've looked at the varied nature of sustainability, its critical relevance, and sustainable business strategies that may lead to long-term success in this last chapter.

Whether you're an experienced company owner or a budding entrepreneur, including sustainability in your business plan might be your ticket to long-term success in an ever-changing and competitive business world.